PHONICS
YEAR 1

Ages 5–6

■SCHOLASTIC

Author Helen Betts

Editorial team Rachel Morgan, Audrey Stokes,
Kate Pedlar, Gemma Smith

Typesetting QBS Learning

Illustration Jim Peacock

Cover design Dipa Mistry

App development Hannah Barnett, Phil Crothers
and RAIOSOFT International Pvt Ltd

Designed using Adobe InDesign

Published in the UK by Scholastic Education, 2020
Book End, Range Road, Witney, Oxfordshire, OX29 0YD
A division of Scholastic Limited
London – New York – Toronto – Sydney – Auckland
Mexico City – New Delhi – Hong Kong
SCHOLASTIC and associated logos are trademarks and/or
registered trademarks of Scholastic Inc.
www.scholastic.co.uk
© 2020 Scholastic Limited
1 2 3 4 5 6 7 8 9   0 1 2 3 4 5 6 7 8 9

British Library Cataloguing-in-Publication Data
A catalogue record for this book is available from the
British Library.

ISBN 978-1407-18347-3

Printed and bound by Ashford Colour Press
Papers used by Scholastic Limited are made from wood
grown in sustainable forests.

Due to the nature of the web, we cannot guarantee the
content or links of any site mentioned.

Every effort has been made to trace copyright holders for the
works reproduced in this book, and the publishers apologise
for any inadvertent omissions.

Note from the publisher:
Please use this product in conjunction with the official
specification and sample assessment materials. Ask your
teacher if you are unsure where to find them.

Contents

How to use this book

This book contains ten different phonics checks for Year 1. As a whole, the complete set of checks provides broad coverage of the test framework for this age group.

Phonics checks

The phonics checks provide practice for the National Phonics Screening Check that children complete towards the end of Year 1. These checks are designed to test a child's knowledge of phonics and require children to read single words aloud. More information on conducting these checks can be found on page 5 and information on marking them is on page 57.

Completing the checks

It is intended that children will take approximately ten minutes to complete each check, but this should not be strictly timed.

After your child has completed a check, mark it and together identify and practise any areas where your child is not confident. Ask them to complete the next check at a later date, when you feel they have had enough time to practise and improve.

Phonics checks guidance

Phonics screening checks: guidance for parents and carers

The phonics screening checks are designed to test a child's knowledge of phonics as one of the building blocks in learning to read and spell. For this purpose, pseudo-words (nonsense words) are used, as a child has to rely on his or her phonic knowledge to read them.

Complete each phonics screening check individually with your child. Introduce the check, as follows:

- I am going to ask you to read some words out loud.

- Some of these words will be new and some you will have seen before.

- Some of the words are not real words but names of imaginary creatures. There is a picture of the creature next to it.

- I will tell you each time you read words that are not real.

Point to each word in turn, for your child to read out loud. Record your child's response to each word, noting if they say it correctly or incorrectly, with comments against incorrect answers; for example, note if your child reads some sounds in the word correctly, but not all, or if your child tries to give a real word instead of a nonsense word. During the phonics check, point to whole words, but do not point in a way that supports the decoding of the word. For example, do not point to individual letters or groups of letters such as 'g' or 'sh'.

Guidance on how to mark the checks can be found on pages 57 to 62.

Phonics activities

Sound detectives

Encourage your child to spot letters and sounds all around them, for example, on signs in the local environment, in their reading book or on food packaging. Each time they spot a particular letter combination or sound, ask them whether they can think of any other words with that sound. Cut out words from old magazines or food wrappers and start a 'word wall' on a sheet of paper, grouping words according to their common sounds and adding others of your own.

Create a creature!

Play around with non-words. Ask your child to draw a picture of an imaginary creature and then give it a name (such as 'splurf'). Encourage them to use the phonics they have been learning, for example, by trying to include a long vowel sound such as 'ay'. Take the game a step further and invent new words for the creature's arms, legs, eyes and body!

I Spy (with a difference)

Play *I Spy* with your child, but not just using initial sounds (such as 's' – 'slipper'). Instead, say, for example, "I spy something beginning with a 'sl' sound", to encourage your child to think about consonant blends. You could also play the game with vowel sounds: for example, "I spy something that has the 'ee' sound."

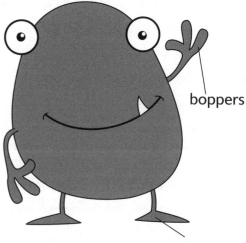

Splurf

boppers

plimbs

Marks

1.

fub

1

2.

lep

1

3.

zot

1

4.

ast

1

Marks

5.

chig

1

6.

jeek

1

7.

hosh

1

8.

quard

1

Marks

9.

crex

1

10.

snith

1

11.

paft

1

12.

morks

1

10 MINS

Marks

13.

hung

1

14.

thick

1

15.

void

1

16.

null

1

10 MINS

17.

broom

1

18.

gloss

1

19.

yelp

1

20.

chant

1

Check 2

Marks

1.

hix

1

2.

vad

1

3.

jom

1

4.

uft

1

5.

sheb

1

6.

yiff

1

7.

quang

1

8.

cheem

1

Marks

9.

skut

1

10.

glort

1

11.

noids

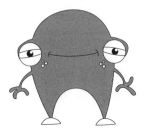

1

12.

themp

1

Marks

13.

lock

1

14.

carp

1

15.

quill

1

16.

shook

1

10 MINS

Marks

17.

broth

1

18.

frizz

1

19.

horns

1

20.

wept

1

Check 3

Marks

1.

wug

1

2.

lan

1

3.

yem

1

4.

isk

1

Marks

5.

hesh

1

6.

zood

1

7.

chiff

1

8.

bazz

1

Marks

9.

flarp

1

10.

cruss

1

11.

vant

1

12.

quomp

1

Marks

13.

wing

1

14.

feed

1

15.

shock

1

16.

thorn

1

Marks

17.

grub

1

18.

spoil

1

19.

jest

1

20.

harms

1

Marks

1.

peb

1

2.

fom

1

3.

vud

1

4.

igs

1

Marks

5.

yeet

1

6.

chax

1

7.

tholl

1

8.

shork

1

10 MINS

Marks

9.

glap

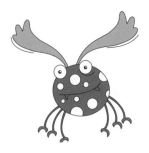

1

10.

cleck

1

11.

roist

1

12.

hask

1

Marks

13.

quiz

1

14.

cuff

1

15.

wool

1

16.

moss

1

10 MINS

Marks

17.

scarf

_____

1

18.

bring

_____

1

19.

jeeps

_____

1

20.

chunk

1

Check 5

Marks

1.

yit

1

2.

zan

1

3.

rog

1

4.

usk

1

Marks

5.

vesh

 1

6.

tharm

 1

7.

cheb

 1

8.

huzz

 1

10 MINS

Marks

9.

cloof

1

10.

prux

1

11.

wilk

1

12.

queft

1

Marks

13.

than

1

14.

such

1

15.

toss

1

16.

shoot

1

Marks

17.

drip

1

18.

snort

1

19.

feeds

1

20.

joint

1

Marks

1.

yoaf

1

2.

hibe

1

3.

quair

1

4.

flirm

1

Marks

5.

shrent

1

6.

glund

1

7.

scray

1

8.

splume

1

<10 MINS>

Marks

9.

weak

1

10.

phone

1

11.

hawks

1

12.

throng

1

Marks

13.

tramp

1

14.

claims

1

15.

spree

1

16.

strict

1

10 MINS

Marks

17.

enjoy

1

18.

rather

1

19.

highest

1

20.

clueless

1

Marks

1.

jorm

1

2.

chabe

1

3.

vur

1

4.

thriff

1

10 MINS

Marks

5.

twunk

1

6.

glaunt

1

7.

sprax

1

8.

scrow

1

Marks

9.

germ

1

10.

cube

1

11.

hair

1

12.

field

1

10 MINS

13.

dreads

1

14.

shrunk

1

15.

splat

1

16.

strive

1

10 MINS

Marks

17.

outer

1

18.

nephew

1

19.

beholds

1

20.

whizzing

1

Marks

1.

zaif

1

2.

quobe

1

3.

jigh

1

4.

shruck

1

 10 MINS

Marks

5.

troaks

 1

6.

fleaps

1

7.

splaw

1

8.

scrox

 1

10
MINS

Marks

9.

soup

1

10.

theme

1

11.

thrill

1

12.

place

1

Marks

13.

grind

1

14.

twirls

1

15.

sprig

1

16.

strand

1

Marks

17.

untie

1

18.

rescue

1

19.

chemist

1

20.

armchair

1

Check 9

Marks

1.

hube

1

2.

quede

1

3.

voy

1

4.

joods

1

Marks

5.

groft

1

6.

phrink

1

7.

sprice

1

8.

scrulk

1

9.

coax

Marks

1

10.

lied

1

11.

thrash

1

12.

brown

1

Marks

13.

blurts

 1

14.

shrimp

 1

15.

scrape

 1

16.

stray

 1

Marks

17.

unite

1

18.

golden

1

19.

rewinds

1

20.

haunting

1

Marks

1.

joil

1

2.

vird

1

3.

zigh

1

4.

clobe

1

Marks

5.

flaint

 1

6.

shrand

 1

7.

spraw

 1

8.

splink

 1

10
MINS

Marks

9.

chute

1

10.

wage

1

11.

due

1

12.

plump

1

10 MINS

Marks

13.

grief

1

14.

elbow

1

15.

screw

1

16.

stroke

1

10 MINS

Marks

17.

throbs

1

18.

crayon

1

19.

whisker

1

20.

shoulder

1

Phonics checks guidance

Marking the check

The following key points should be remembered when scoring the check. Score one mark for each correct word read.

- Children may sound out parts of the word before reading the whole word, but this is optional.
- Children may stretch the phonemes (single letter sounds, or combination of letter sounds) but as long as they blend correctly to pronounce the word, a mark may be awarded.
- Alternative pronunciations should be considered for pseudo-words if the sounds exist in other words, for example: a soft 'g' or hard 'g' sound in 'ged' – see further guidance on pages 58 to 62.
- A child's accent should be taken into account and not disadvantage him or her. Similarly, if a child has particular speech difficulties, for example, in pronouncing 'th', this should be taken into account.
- If a child makes an incorrect attempt but then corrects it, this should be marked as correct.

In the National Phonics Screening Check, there are two sections. Section 2 has more complex words than Section 1. The full check has 40 words across the two sections and children need to read at least 32 words correctly.

In this book, each check contains 20 words and so children should be achieving around 16 words per check. However, Checks 1 to 5 are similar to Section 1 of the national check and Checks 6 to 10 are more similar to Section 2 (the harder part).

Therefore, it is likely that your child will find Checks 1 to 5 easier and so may score higher in these than in Checks 6 to 10. The target of 16 should be treated as a rough guide only; if you have any concerns, please speak to your child's teacher.

Answers

Check 1

Score one mark for each correct word read.

Pseudo-words	Acceptable pronunciations
1. fub	This item uses the 'f' from 'fib' and rhymes with 'hub'.
2. lep	This item uses the 'l' from 'leg' and rhymes with 'step'.
3. zot	This item uses the 'z' from 'zip' and rhymes with 'dot'.
4. ast	This item uses the 'a' from 'and' and rhymes with 'past'.
5. chig	This item uses the 'ch' from 'chip' and rhymes with 'dig'.
6. jeek	This item uses the 'j' from 'jet' and rhymes with 'peek'.
7. hosh	This item uses the 'h' from 'head' and rhymes with 'gosh'.
8. quard	This item uses the 'qu' from 'quick' and rhymes with 'hard'.
9. crex	This item uses the 'cr' from 'crib' and rhymes with 'vex'.
10. snith	This item uses the 'sn' from 'snail' and rhymes with 'pith' or 'with'.
11. paft	This item uses the 'p' from 'pan' and rhymes with 'raft'.
12. morks	This item uses the 'm' from 'mop' and rhymes with 'forks'.

Real words
13. hung
14. thick
15. void
16. null
17. broom
18. gloss
19. yelp
20. chant

Check 2

Score one mark for each correct word read.

Pseudo-words	Acceptable pronunciations
1. hix	This item uses the 'h' from 'head' and rhymes with 'fix'.
2. vad	This item uses the 'v' from 'van' and rhymes with 'bad'.
3. jom	This item uses the 'j' from 'jet' and rhymes with 'from'.
4. uft	This item uses the 'u' from 'under' and rhymes with 'tuft'.
5. sheb	This item uses the 'sh' from 'shop' and rhymes with 'web'.
6. yiff	This item uses the 'y' from 'you' and rhymes with 'sniff'.
7. quang	This item uses the 'qu' from 'quick' and rhymes with 'fang'.
8. cheem	This item uses the 'ch' from 'chip' and rhymes with 'seem'.
9. skut	This item uses the 'sk' from 'skin' and rhymes with 'hut'.
10. glort	This item uses the 'gl' from 'glad' and rhymes with 'sort'.
11. noids	This item uses the 'n' from 'nap' and rhymes with 'voids'.
12. themp	This item uses the 'th' from 'this' or 'thing' and rhymes with 'hemp'.

Real words
13. lock
14. carp
15. quill
16. shook
17. broth
18. frizz
19. horns
20. wept

Check 3

Score one mark for each correct word read.

Pseudo-words	Acceptable pronunciations	Real words
1. wug	This item uses the 'w' from 'web' and rhymes with 'tug'.	13. wing
2. lan	This item uses the 'l' from 'leg' and rhymes with 'pan'.	14. feed
3. yem	This item uses the 'y' from 'you' and rhymes with 'hem'.	15. shock
4. isk	This item uses the 'i' from 'insect' and rhymes with 'risk'.	16. thorn
5. hesh	This item uses the 'h' from 'head' and rhymes with 'mesh'.	17. grub
6. zood	This item uses the 'z' from 'zip' and rhymes with 'good' or 'food'.	18. spoil
7. chiff	This item uses the 'ch' from 'chip' and rhymes with 'sniff'.	19. jest
8. bazz	This item uses the 'b' from 'bug' and rhymes with 'jazz'.	20. harms
9. flarp	This item uses the 'fl' from 'flat' and rhymes with 'harp'.	
10. cruss	This item uses the 'cr' from 'crib' and rhymes with 'fuss'.	
11. vant	This item uses the 'v' from 'van' and rhymes with 'rant'.	
12. quomp	This item uses the 'qu' from 'quick' and rhymes with 'stomp'.	

Check 4

Score one mark for each correct word read.

Pseudo-words	Acceptable pronunciations	Real words
1. peb	This item uses the 'p' from 'pan' and rhymes with 'web'.	13. quiz
2. fom	This item uses the 'f' from 'fib' and rhymes with 'from'.	14. cuff
3. vud	This item uses the 'v' from 'van' and rhymes with 'mud'.	15. wool
4. igs	This item uses the 'i' from 'insect' and rhymes with 'twigs'.	16. moss
5. yeet	This item uses the 'y' from 'you' and rhymes with 'feet'.	17. scarf
6. chax	This item uses the 'ch' from 'chip' and rhymes with 'fax'.	18. bring
7. tholl	This item uses the 'th' from 'this' or 'thing' and rhymes with 'doll'.	19. jeeps
8. shork	This item uses the 'sh' from 'shop' and rhymes with 'fork'.	20. chunk
9. glap	This item uses the 'gl' from 'glad' and rhymes with 'map'.	
10. cleck	This item uses the 'cl' from 'clap' and rhymes with 'deck'.	
11. roist	This item uses the 'r' from 'run' and rhymes with 'hoist'.	
12. hask	This item uses the 'h' from 'head' and rhymes with 'task'.	

Check 5

Score one mark for each correct word read.

Pseudo-words	Acceptable pronunciations	Real words
1. yit	This item uses the 'y' from 'you' and rhymes with 'sit'.	13. than
2. zan	This item uses the 'z' from 'zip' and rhymes with 'pan'.	14. such
3. rog	This item uses the 'r' from 'run' and rhymes with 'dog'.	15. toss
4. usk	This item uses the 'u' from 'under' and rhymes with 'tusk'.	16. shoot
5. vesh	This item uses the 'v' from 'van' and rhymes with 'mesh'.	17. drip
6. tharm	This item uses the 'th' from 'this' or 'thing' and rhymes with 'arm'.	18. snort
7. cheb	This item uses the 'ch' from 'chip' and rhymes with 'web'.	19. feeds
8. huzz	This item uses the 'h' from 'head' and rhymes with 'buzz'.	20. joint
9. cloof	This item uses the 'cl' from 'click' and rhymes with 'hoof' or 'woof'.	
10. prux	This item uses the 'pr' from 'print' and rhymes with 'crux'.	
11. wilk	This item uses the 'w' from 'web' and rhymes with 'milk'.	
12. queft	This item uses the 'qu' from 'quick' and rhymes with 'left'.	

Check 6

Score one mark for each correct word read.

Pseudo-words	Acceptable pronunciations	Real words
1. yoaf	This item uses the 'y' from 'you' and rhymes with 'loaf'.	9. weak
2. hibe	This item uses the 'h' from 'head' and rhymes with 'jibe'.	10. phone
3. quair	This item uses the 'qu' from 'quick' and rhymes with 'fair'.	11. hawks
4. flirm	This item uses the 'fl' from 'flat' and rhymes with 'firm'.	12. throng
5. shrent	This item uses the 'shr' from 'shrimp' and rhymes with 'went'.	13. tramp
6. glund	This item uses the 'gl' from 'glad' and rhymes with 'fund'.	14. claims
7. scray	This item uses the 'scr' from 'scrap' and rhymes with 'pay'.	15. spree
8. splume	This item uses the 'spl' from 'splat' and rhymes with 'fume'.	16. strict
		17. enjoy
		18. rather
		19. highest
		20. clueless

Check 7

Score one mark for each correct word read.

Pseudo-words	Acceptable pronunciations	Real words
1. jorm	This item uses the 'j' from 'jet' and rhymes with 'form'.	9. germ
2. chabe	This item uses the 'ch' from 'chip' or 'chef' and rhymes with 'babe'.	10. cube
3. vur	This item uses the 'v' from 'van' and rhymes with 'fur'.	11. hair
4. thriff	This item uses the 'thr' from 'throw' and rhymes with 'tiff'.	12. field
5. twunk	This item uses the 'tw' from 'twin' and rhymes with 'bunk'.	13. dreads
6. glaunt	This item uses the 'gl' from 'glad' and rhymes with 'haunt'.	14. shrunk
7. sprax	This item uses the 'spr' from 'spray' and rhymes with 'tax'.	15. splat
8. scrow	This item uses the 'scr' from 'scrap' and rhymes with 'cow' or 'low'.	16. strive
		17. outer
		18. nephew
		19. beholds
		20. whizzing

Check 8

Score one mark for each correct word read.

Pseudo-words	Acceptable pronunciations	Real words
1. zaif	This item uses the 'z' from 'zip' and rhymes with 'waif'.	9. soup
2. quobe	This item uses the 'qu' from 'quick' and rhymes with 'robe'.	10. theme
3. jigh	This item uses the 'j' from 'jet' and rhymes with 'sigh'.	11. thrill
4. shruck	This item uses the 'shr' from 'shrimp' and rhymes with 'duck'.	12. place
5. troaks	This item uses the 'tr' from 'tree' and rhymes with 'soaks'.	13. grind
6. fleaps	This item uses the 'fl' from 'flat' and rhymes with 'heaps'.	14. twirls
7. splaw	This item uses the 'spl' from 'splat' and rhymes with 'paw'.	15. sprig
8. scrox	This item uses the 'scr' from 'scrap' and rhymes with 'fox'.	16. strand
		17. untie
		18. rescue
		19. chemist
		20. armchair

Check 9

Score one mark for each correct word read.

Pseudo-words	Acceptable pronunciations	Real words
1. hube	This item uses the 'h' from 'head' and rhymes with 'cube' or 'lube'.	9. coax
2. quede	This item uses the 'qu' from 'quick' and rhymes with 'swede'.	10. lied
3. voy	This item uses the 'v' from 'van' and rhymes with 'toy'.	11. thrash
4. joods	This item uses the 'j' from 'jet' and rhymes with 'goods' or 'foods'.	12. brown
5. groft	This item uses the 'gr' from 'grin' and rhymes with 'soft'.	13. blurts
6. phrink	This item uses the 'phr' from 'phrase' and rhymes with 'sink'.	14. shrimp
7. sprice	This item uses the 'spr' from 'spray' and rhymes with 'mice'.	15. scrape
8. scrulk	This item uses the 'scr' from 'scrap' and rhymes with 'bulk'.	16. stray
		17. unite
		18. golden
		19. rewinds
		20. haunting

Check 10

Score one mark for each correct word read.

Pseudo-words	Acceptable pronunciations	Real words
1. joil	This item uses the 'j' from 'jet' and rhymes with 'soil'.	9. chute
2. vird	This item uses the 'v' from 'van' and rhymes with 'bird'.	10. wage
3. zigh	This item uses the 'z' from 'zip' and rhymes with 'sigh'.	11. due
4. clobe	This item uses the 'cl' from 'clock' and rhymes with 'robe'.	12. plump
5. flaint	This item uses the 'fl' from 'flat' and rhymes with 'paint'.	13. grief
6. shrand	This item uses the 'shr' from 'shrimp' and rhymes with 'hand'.	14. elbow
7. spraw	This item uses the 'spr' from 'spray' and rhymes with 'law'.	15. screw
8. splink	This item uses the 'spl' from 'splash' and rhymes with 'sink'.	16. stroke
		17. throbs
		18. crayon
		19. whisker
		20. shoulder

Progress chart

Fill in your score in the table below to see how well you've done.

	Score	Percentage
Check 1	/20	
Check 2	/20	
Check 3	/20	
Check 4	/20	
Check 5	/20	
Check 6	/20	
Check 7	/20	
Check 8	/20	
Check 9	/20	
Check 10	/20	

Percentage	
0–33%	Good try! You need more practice in some areas – ask an adult to help you.
34–69%	You're doing really well. Ask for extra help for any areas you found tricky.
70–100%	You're a 10-Minute SATs Test phonics star – good work!

Reward Certificate

Well done!

You have completed all of the 10-Minute SATs Tests

Name: _____   Date: _____

10 MINUTE SATs TESTS
QUICK TESTS FOR SATs SUCCESS

BOOST YOUR CHILD'S CONFIDENCE WITH 10-MINUTE SATs TESTS

Bite-size mini SATs tests which take just 10 minutes to complete

Covers key National Test topics

Full answers and progress chart provided to track improvement

Available for Years 1 to 6

FIND OUT MORE
WWW.SCHOLASTIC.CO.UK